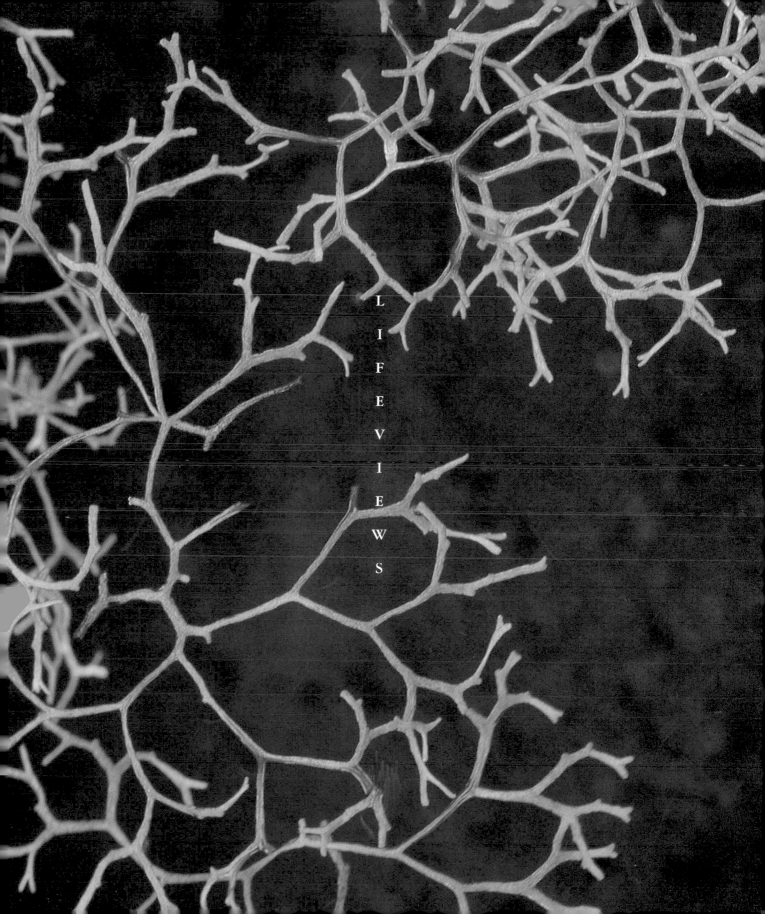

L
I
F
E

V
I
E
W
S

Published by Creative Education
123 South Broad Street, Mankato, Minnesota 56001
Creative Education is an imprint of The Creative Company

Art direction by Rita Marshall; Production design by The Design Lab/Kathy Petelinsek
Photographs by David Liebman

Library of Congress Cataloging-in-Publication Data

Halfmann, Janet. Life in a pond / by Janet Halfmann; p. cm. — (LifeViews) Includes index
Summary: Briefly describes some of the creatures that live in a pond, including water striders, tadpoles,
and dragonfly nymphs. Suggests several related activities.
ISBN 1-58341-073-2
1. Pond animals—Juvenile literature. 2. Pond ecology—Juvenile literature. 3. Ponds.
[1. Pond animals. 2. Pond ecology. 3. Ecology.] I. Title. II. Series: LifeViews (Mankato, Minn.)
QL146.H34   2000
591.763'6—dc21   99-10295

First Edition

2   4   6   8   9   7   5   3   1

LIFE IN A
POND

JANET HALFMANN

PHOTOGRAPHS BY DAVID LIEBMAN

SMALL, still bodies of fresh water, called **ponds**, are found all over the world. A pond's ecosystem is like a two-story house with a flat roof. On the watery roof live the floating animals and those that can walk on the surface film. Below the water's surface are animals that swim or drift. On the muddy or sandy floor level, bottom feeders prowl. Everywhere, creatures are skating, swimming, paddling, or lurking to get their next meal. Ponds are usually shallow enough for sunlight to reach to the bottom, which means that plants grow at all levels of the pond as well. Many fascinating plants and animals interact to make the calm waters of a pond their home.

Plants such as pickerel weed brighten the pond edge.

Water striders skate across the surface film of the pond on their long spidery legs, leaving dimples in the water with their feet. These tiny, slender black insects, with bodies about the size of a grain of rice, are one of the most visible creatures on the pond. They live almost their entire lives on the pond's surface film—a kind of thin elastic sheet of **air** that covers the water. With a body like a boat, the water strider's long middle legs are like oars, while the two hind legs steer. These sprawling legs spread the bug's weight over a large area, making it light enough to walk on water. The water strider also has thick pads of tiny, oily hairs on its feet that help keep it afloat.

Groups of water striders, also known as pond skaters, patrol the surface of the pond, looking for ants and other prey insects that fall into the water. The water strider knows immediately when an insect hits the water by the **ripples** it makes. The water strider skates over and grabs the insect with the claws on its short front legs. It uses one pair of sharp **stylets** to pierce the hard body of the insect prey; then it

Water striders often group together in large numbers. Some species can survive in fast-moving water. All water striders are found in freshwater, with only one exception, a kind called Halobates.

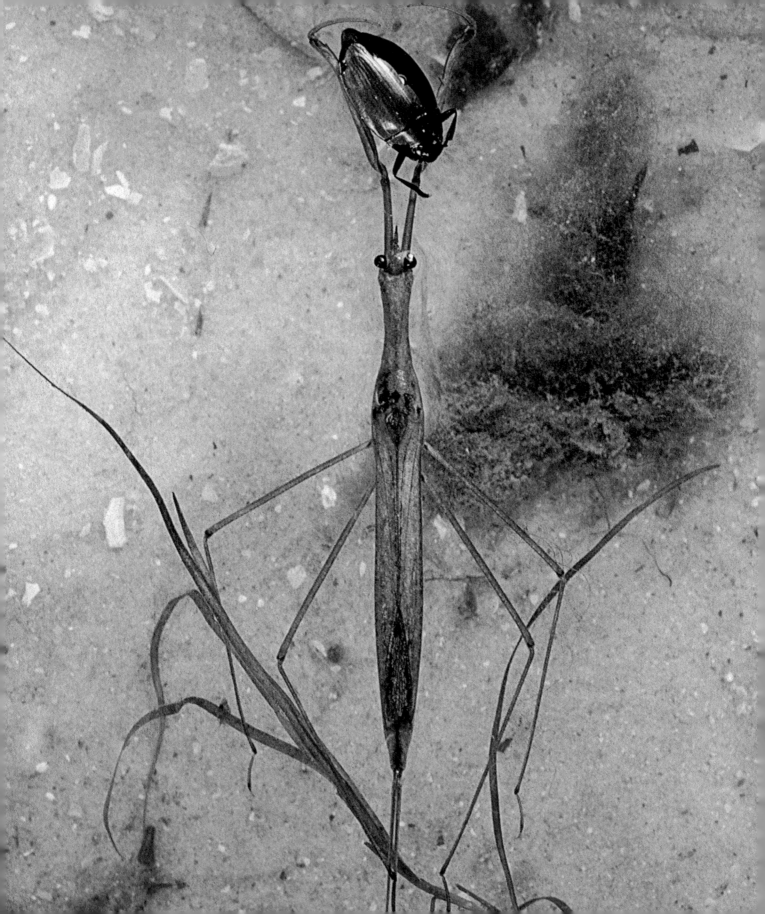

uses a second tube-like pair to consume the food as if slurping through a straw. Sometimes the water strider leaps into the air to catch prey.

When water striders sense danger with their large eyes or by ripples in the water, they scurry to find shelter. They can even hide below the surface of the water for a time, breathing air trapped in their body hairs. Animals that prey on water striders include birds, fish, and dragonflies.

Another fascinating pond bug is the **water scorpion**. It has two long half-tubes at its tail end that lock together to form a breathing tube. The bug hangs upside down on a water plant and sticks the tip of its breathing tube out of the water, drawing air into spaces beneath its wings. These breathing tubes resemble tiny snorkels sticking up through the water's surface.

The water scorpion does not hunt. It is a poor swimmer, so it must wait for an insect, **tadpole**, or small fish to swim near. When this happens, the water scorpion grabs the prey in its front legs, which then snap shut like a

The water scorpion (opposite) has a huge appetite for minnows, frogs, and other aquatic insects. It strikes so quickly that its prey seldom sees it coming.

jackknife. The water scorpion's beak punctures the prey, and it is consumed.

Some water scorpions are long and slender like twigs, while others resemble leaves. If captured or handled, a water scorpion will pretend to be dead. Although the water scorpion got its name because its breathing tube resembles the tail of a land scorpion, the two creatures are not related.

In the ooze at the bottom of the pond, the **water boatman** feeds by scooping diatoms, algae, and tiny animals into its mouth with its short, hairy front legs. When this pea-sized bug needs a new air supply, it floats to the surface. There it traps air under its wings and in tiny hairs on its body. This gives the boatman a silvery glow. A good swimmer, the boatman paddles back to the bottom of the pond using its fringed back legs as oars.

The water boatman is just one of many pond animals that rely on tiny plantlike organisms such as **algae** to stay alive. The plentiful one-celled algae are perhaps the most important living things in the pond. Algae are

The light-colored backswimmer (opposite top) can be as small as 0.08 inches (2 mm) or up to .7 inches (17 mm) in length. Though deadly to small prey, the backswimmer's bite causes only mild pain. The pond snail (opposite bottom) varies in size as well.

relatives of diatoms and amoebas, which are also vital to life in a pond. Like members of the plant kingdom, algae make food using energy from the sun. Food made by algae is passed along to the water boatman and other insects, which in turn are eaten by larger pond animals. Algae is important because it is the first link in the pond's **food chain**. Without it, many animals would be without food. Algae also helps produce the oxygen needed to keep the pond alive.

Unlike plants, algae don't have roots, stems, or leaves, nor do they grow from seeds. Green algae is the most plentiful kind, with 6,500 species. A common one is **Spirogyra**, which forms long chains. It is also known as pond scum, water-silk, or mermaid's tresses, because of its hairlike strands. Each microscopic cell in the Spirogyra chain is a short, transparent tube with a spiral of green bands inside. The bands contain the green pigment called **chlorophyll**, which allows the algae to use sunlight to make food. A sticky slime covers the chains to protect them.

Spirogyra divide in two, creating longer and longer

Wolfia (opposite) is the smallest plant in the world.

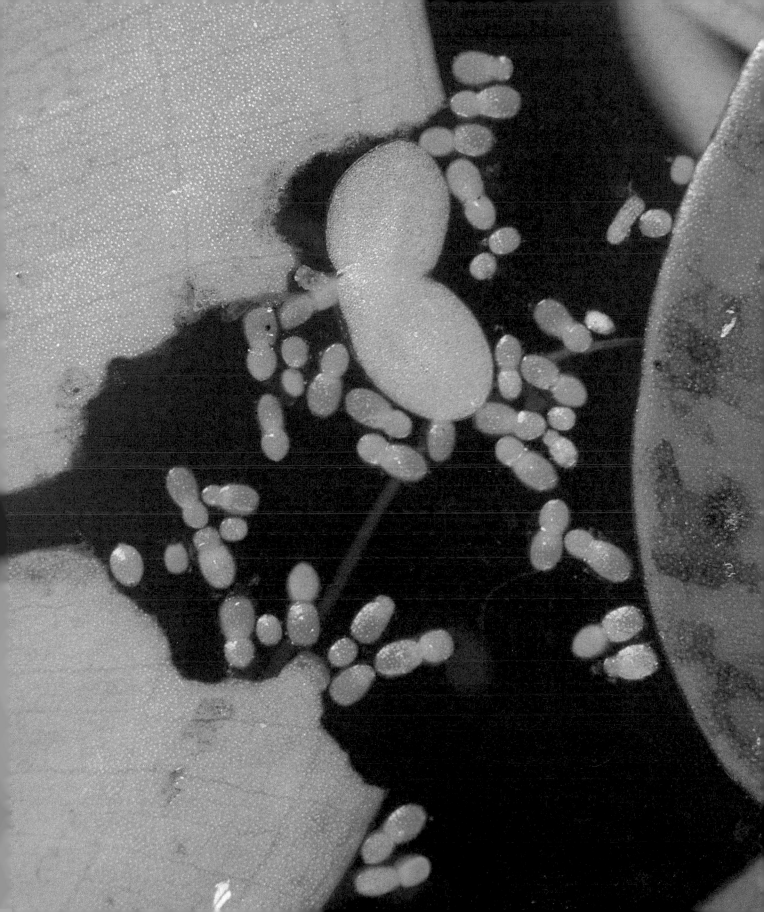

chains that form a soft blanket on the water's surface. During the day, the tiny chains are kept afloat by air bubbles produced while the algae makes food. At night, when there is no sunlight, the algae sink.

Another kind of green algae in the pond is called **Euglena**. It acts like a plant, using energy from the sun to make food. But strangely, Euglena wiggles through the water like an animal. It swims rapidly by thrashing the long whip, called a flagellum, located on its front end.

A single Euglena is so small that it is invisible to the human eye, but a swarm can create scum on top of a pond. All of the 150 species of Euglenas look like tiny green pea pods. By splitting in half lengthwise, one creature can create many copies of itself in a short time. If a pond dries up, many species can enclose themselves in a tough casing and rest until water returns.

Floating just below the pond's surface are silvery rafts of jelly: **frog eggs**. About 10 days after the eggs are laid, baby

The tadpole (opposite top) and Northern cricket frog (opposite below) are near the top of the pond food chain. They eat many species of insects, including flower fly larvae.

frogs, called tadpoles, wriggle out of the jelly. Tadpoles don't look anything like their parents. Instead, they look like fish. They have long, fin-like tails for swimming, feathery gills for breathing underwater, and no legs.

The newly hatched tadpoles, also called **polliwogs**, eat algae and other plants. Gradually, the tadpole grows back legs, and then front legs. At this stage, the tadpole starts to eat tiny animals. Its gills disappear and it develops lungs, which means it must swim to the surface of the pond to breathe air.

The smallest tadpoles are almost too tiny to be seen, while the largest— Bullfrog tadpoles—grow to seven inches (18 cm) in length. When a tadpole is about ready to leave the pond, it stops eating. It lives off the nutrients stored in its tail, which shrinks away. Its mouth and eyes get bigger. This change from a tadpole to a frog is called **metamorphosis**. Many kinds of tadpoles, such as those of the Wood Frog and Spring Peeper, change into

The pond attracts many strange insects. The damselfly (bottom left and right) is one example. Others include dragonfly nymphs (bottom center) and large, full-grown dragonflies (top).

frogs in a few weeks. Others, such as the Green Frog and Bullfrog, may take up to a year.

Another water-borne creature is so ferocious that it's known as a "pond monster." The **dragonfly nymph** doesn't look anything like its colorful, flying parents. This tiny, rather ugly bug has a big head and mouth, gills for breathing, six legs, and no wings. It has a long lip that shoots out with lightning speed to grab unsuspecting prey that venture near its hiding place at the bottom of the pond. Hooks on the end of the lip grab the prey and bring it back to the nymph's mouth. Dragonfly nymphs eat just about anything, from other insects to tadpoles and small fish.

To speed away from enemies, the dragonfly nymph squeezes water out of its gill chamber, pushing it forward. A Common Green Darner nymph can move 20 inches (51 cm) per second.

Nymphs live in the pond for one to two years, depending on the species. When it reaches about two inches (5 cm) long,

Water bugs spend their entire lives—from larva to adult—in water. These insects are also called water beetles or diving beetles. About 4,000 species make up the family called Dytiscidae.

the nymph stops eating and crawls up a plant, log, or rock. At night, its skin splits and the new winged adult emerges. When the sun comes up, the **dragonfly** stretches its wings and flies away from the pond.

In about a month, dragonflies return to the pond to mate. They fly over the pond attached together. Then their abdomens form a circle shape called a mating wheel. The female lays her eggs in or near the water as the male guards her from enemies. In less than a month, the eggs hatch into a new group of "pond monsters."

Another monster of the pond is the tiny stinging **hydra**. This strange creature, if cut into several pieces, will grow a new animal from each section. It gets its name from Hydra, the legendary nine-headed monster from Greek myths.

Hydras usually stay in one place, but they can move. One way they do this is by rolling like a ball along the bottom of the pond. When threatened, the hydra squeezes itself into a tiny pinhead-sized blob. Hydras can be white, pink, tan,

The pond is home to a seemingly infinite variety of plants, flowers, insects, lizards, and birds. All life in a pond is interconnected. Each creature has an important role to play in the pond's web of life.

brown, or green. The **Green Hydra** gets its color from algae that live inside its body.

The hydra looks like a short piece of frayed string. The frayed ends are actually stinging **tentacles** surrounding the hydra's mouth. The hydra anchors the foot end of its tubelike body to rocks and water plants, then waits for tiny animals to swim near. It often eats newly hatched tadpoles or water fleas. When an animal brushes against the tentacles, tiny poisoned harpoons shoot out and paralyze the victim so the hydra can eat it.

One type of **flatworm** actually eats the hydra's stinging cells. There are about 13,000 species of flatworms. The most common flatworms in ponds are called **planarians**. Shorter than a paper clip, they look like tiny, flat arrows the color of mud. Two **eyespots** on their heads tell light from dark. Trillions of tiny hairs cover a planarian's body. They beat like tiny oars to help move the worm along a track of slime.

The worm's mouth is on its underside, near the middle

Turtles, newts, and salamanders may prey on snails and their eggs. Newts can live in the water and only periodically come up for air. Land-dwelling salamanders need a moist habitat; in fact, they may bury themselves in mud at the water's edge.

of its body. The planarian traps its prey with slime, then wraps its body around it. A long tube called a **pharynx** shoots out of its mouth and consumes the prey. Planarians feed on both dead animals and tiny living animals such as insect larvae.

Planarians reproduce in a variety of ways. One species anchors its tail to something, then crawls forward until its body breaks in two. Each half then grows into a complete worm. Planarians also produce eggs. They put them in a protective case called a **cocoon** and attach them to rocks or plants. Those laid in the summer hatch within a few weeks into young worms resembling their parents. Eggs laid in the fall usually don't hatch until spring.

No matter what the season, the pond is home to an amazing variety of plants and animals, each with a unique way of eating, breathing, and creating new life. From the tiniest algae to the large croaking Bullfrog, each is an important part of the pond community.

Crayfish can be white, gray, brown…even blue or transparent!

A POND IN YOUR HOME

You can set up a small home for frogs and other pond dwellers that recreates their natural environment. Many frogs need a home that is part land and part water, known as a semiaquatic terrarium, aqua-terrarium, or vivarium.

You Will Need

- 10-gallon or larger plastic or glass aquarium tank with a screen cover
- Large, shallow glass or plastic container
- Water without chlorine (use tap water left sitting at room temperature for at least a day, or bottled mineral spring water)
- Smooth pebbles
- Peat moss or dead leaves
- Potting soil
- Land and water plants
- Moss, stones, bark, small logs, small clay pots, and other habitat materials

Setup

1. Set the tank on a sturdy table or shelf in a bright place, but not in direct sunlight.
2. Set the shallow container (pond area) in a corner of the tank.

To Create The Land Area

1. Put about two inches (5 cm) of washed smooth pebbles or other drainage material on the bottom of the tank.
2. Add a layer of peat moss or dead leaves.
3. Add potting soil. Shape it into small hills and valleys and slope it gently toward the pond. Put flat, smooth stones or moss around the pond edge of the land area. (Make sure the shallow container can be removed easily for cleaning.)
4. In the soil, put plants such as ferns, mosses, and seedling trees.
5. Add small rocks, bark, moss, small branches or logs, and small overturned clay pots to give your animals places to climb and hide. Make sure there are no sharp edges anywhere that could injure the animals.

6. Water the soil well, but don't make it soggy. Mist the plants and container daily, and water the plants once a week. Be sure to use water without chlorine.

Note: For a simpler setup, just put peat moss in the land area, and use potted plants.

To Create The Water Area

1. Put one inch (2.5 cm) of washed, smooth pebbles in the bottom of the shallow container.
2. Anchor water plants such as elodea in the pebbles and add some floating water plants, such as water lettuce.
3. Build a ramp from the water to the land with smooth, flat stones or cork bark.
4. Fill the shallow container with water with no chlorine. Semiaquatic frogs need at least two inches (5 cm) of water, and tadpoles need four inches (10 cm).

Clean water is very important to the health of your pond. Whenever the water looks murky, move the animals to another container while you clean the container and change the water.

Pond Animals

Frogs that can live in a semiaquatic terrarium home include most of the typical frogs known as "true frogs," such as the Carpenter Frog and Green Frog. Keep only one species, or kind, of frog in your small home. Other animals to keep in a semiaquatic terrarium include salamanders and newts. Land and pond snails thrive in terrariums, but too many of them can quickly overtake a pond and destroy all the plant life.

Feed frogs, salamanders, and newts small earthworms, crickets, and other live insects. You also may want to add a vitamin-mineral supplement from a pet store. Snails eat algae and other plants. You can feed land snails a bit of lettuce, carrot, or apple.

Collect a few frog eggs and their jelly from a pond, or get them from a biology supply house or pet store. Put the eggs in your pond. When the tadpoles hatch, make sure they aren't crowded. The tadpoles will eat the water plants, and you can feed them small pieces of boiled lettuce or spinach and a pinch of flaked fish food. After the tadpoles grow legs, they need meat, such as live water fleas and gnat and mosquito larvae, or canned dog food or ground beef to which vitamins and minerals have been added. Every day, remove any food the tadpoles don't eat, so it won't decay and poison the water. Change the water often, or remove waste with an aquarium siphon or a meat baster.

Keeping an indoor pond is like having a little piece of nature in your own home or school. Watching the animals is a fun way to learn about ponds.

GROW ALGAE

Algae is very important in a pond because it makes food using energy from the sun. The plant-like algae are eaten by tiny animals, which are in turn eaten by larger animals. Algae grows very fast. Get some algae from a pond and watch it grow!

You Will Need
- Pond water
- Plastic or glass jar
- Magnifying glass or microscope

What To Do
1. Collect pond water in the jar.
2. Set the jar in a warm, sunny spot.
3. Watch the water get greener. That means the plants are growing.
4. Take some of the algae out of the jar and look at it more closely with a magnifying glass or microscope.

Algae At The Science Fair
How important is the sun to algae? You can find out by collecting three jars of pond water. Put one jar in the sun, one in a dark place, and one in the refrigerator. What happens?

LEARN MORE ABOUT PONDS

Adopt-a-Pond
Toronto Zoo
361A Old Finch Avenue
Scarborough, Ontario
Canada M1B 5K7
http://www.torontozoo.com/adoptapond/
   main.html

Center for Global Environmental
Education; A Thousand Friends of Frogs
Hamline University Graduate School,
MS-A1760
1536 Hewitt Avenue
St. Paul, MN 55104-1284
E-mail: frogs@hamline.edu
http://cgee.hamline.edu/FROGS/index.html

National Pond Society
3933 Loch Highland Pass NE
Roswell, GA 30075-2029
E-mail: nps@pondscapes.com
http://www.pondscapes.com/page6.html

Give Water a Hand
216 Agriculture Hall
1450 Linden Drive
Madison, WI 53706
E-mail: erc@uwex.edu
http://www.uwex.edu/erc/index.html

Project WET
201 Culbertson Hall
Montana State University
Bozeman, MT 59717
http://www.montana.edu:80/wwwwet/

Society for the Study of Amphibians
   and Reptiles
c/o George Pisani
Division of Biological Sciences
University of Kansas
Lawrence, KS 66045-2106
http://falcon.cc.ukans.edu/~gpisani/
   SSAR.html

American Zoo and Aquarium Association
8403 Coleville Road
Suite 710
Silver Spring, MD 20910
http:www.aza.org/about/whatisaza.htm

The Nature Conservancy
International Headquarters
4245 North Fairfax Drive
Suite 100
Arlington Virginia 22203-1606
http://www.tnc.org/

INDEX

The pond is teeming with colorful, oddly shaped lifeforms.